THE LIBRARY OF
AMERICAN
LIVES AND TIMES™

ALEXANDER HAMILTON

Federalist
and Founding Father

Lisa DeCarolis

The Rosen Publishing Group's
PowerPlus Books™
New York

For David

Published in 2003 by The Rosen Publishing Group, Inc.
29 East 21st Street, New York, NY 10010

First Edition

Editor's Note: All quotations have been reproduced as they appeared in the letters and diaries from which they were borrowed. No correction was made to the inconsistent spelling that was common in that time period.

Library of Congress Cataloging-in-Publication Data

DeCarolis, Lisa.
  Alexander Hamilton : Federalist and founding father / by Lisa DeCarolis.
  1st ed.
    p. cm. — (Library of American lives and times)
  Includes bibliographical references (p.   ) and index.
  Summary: Surveys the life of Alexander Hamilton, a founding father, later becoming the first Secretary of the Treasury.
  ISBN 0-8239-5735-7 (library binding)
  1. Hamilton, Alexander, 1757–1804—Juvenile literature. 2. Statesmen—United States—Biography—Juvenile literature. 3. United States—Politics and government—1783–1809—Juvenile literature.   [1. Hamilton, Alexander, 1757–1804. 2. Statesmen.]   I. Title. II. Series.
E302.6.H2D35 2003
973.4'092—dc21
[B]

2001004882

Manufactured in the United States of America

CONTENTS

HAMILTON

1. A Little-Known Founding Father

Alexander Hamilton is best known today for his picture on the ten-dollar bill. Surprisingly many Americans mistakenly think that he was a president, like many of the other men whose pictures appear on money. In fact, Hamilton was the first U.S. Secretary of the Treasury. He was also one of the most important American Founding Fathers. If Hamilton was so important, why do we know so little about him? Perhaps it is because a treasury's secretary seems less interesting than does a clever inventor and diplomat, such as Benjamin Franklin. Working with stocks, bonds, and banks does not capture our imaginations like the adventures of a great general such as George Washington. Although Thomas Jefferson's Declaration of Independence is studied throughout the world, Hamilton's dry-sounding *Report on Public Credit*

Opposite: An engraving of Alexander Hamilton appears on every ten-dollar bill. Hamilton became the first secretary of the Treasury in 1789. He put complex financial principles to work for the new U.S. government. As secretary of the treasury, Hamilton introduced plans for a federal bank that would issue paper currency to pay taxes and debts owed by the government. He also introduced plans for the U.S. Mint, which would print money and create coins for the new nation.

is practically unknown, even though it ensured the success of a new nation.

In 1789, when the United States established its permanent form of government, the nation was nearly bankrupt and needed to be bailed out of deep financial troubles. America was fortunate to have someone like Alexander Hamilton in public service. He understood the principles of finance and the necessity of a strong economy for the survival of a new nation. More important, he was able to put those ideas to work in American government.

Hamilton did much more than rescue the economy of the United States, though. He was George Washington's trusted aide during the American Revolution, and he was his closest adviser during Washington's presidency. After the war, Hamilton held office in New York and in the national government. All the while, he was a keen observer of American politics, and he became a leading statesman who argued for a stronger government. His efforts led to the Constitutional Convention of 1787, which achieved that goal. Hamilton then explained and interpreted the Constitution in writings and in speeches that helped gain acceptance for the new government. Were it not for Hamilton and his supporters, the small, troubled nation that emerged from the American Revolution might have fallen into ruin.

The events that led to the American Revolution had a great impact on Hamilton and the other Founding

Fathers. The colonies experienced great prosperity at the time of the French and Indian War (1754–1763), during which England drove the French from most of France's North American lands. After the war, the crown needed funds to pay its war debts and decided to raise the needed money from its colonies. Parliament enacted a series of taxes on the American colonies, beginning with a tax on molasses in 1763. Soon afterward the notorious Stamp Act was passed, which was a sales tax on many commonly used items, such as newspapers, playing cards, and necessary legal documents. The Stamp Act was repealed following riots and protests. The Townshend Acts, in 1767, included a tax on tea, which sent the colonies to the brink of revolution.

These are examples of the stamps that the British government required to appear on virtually all printed materials, including legal and commercial papers, licenses, newspapers, and even playing cards. The Stamp Act caused protests throughout the American colonies.

Paying the taxes was not what most concerned the colonists. They were used to paying taxes to their colonial assemblies, which they considered their true representative governments. The new taxes were different, because they were passed by Parliament and were paid directly to the royal treasury. The colonists claimed that the taxes were unfair, because they had no representative in Parliament like they had in their local assemblies. Up to that time, the colonies had avoided being taxed without their consent. The sudden change in policy made them feel as if they had lost the rights guaranteed to them under the English constitution.

The colonial assemblies pulled together to form the Stamp Act Congress, which petitioned Parliament to repeal the stamp tax. The crisis worsened when Parliament ignored the petitions. The colonies then agreed to boycott the taxed items. The success of these efforts prompted a new outlook among the colonial leaders. The colonies united in a common cause for the first time. The idea that America could be an independent nation began to take shape. The British also saw this and tried to restrict the activities of the colonial assemblies. The colonists grew angrier. They banded together to fight what they felt was the tyranny of the Crown.

Throughout the tax crisis and the revolution that followed, words drove the fight for liberty in America. The colonists debated whether they should rebel or whether they should accept Parliament's policies. Many colonists,

IN CONGRESS, JULY 4, 1776.

A DECLARATION

BY THE REPRESENTATIVES OF THE

UNITED STATES OF AMERICA,

IN GENERAL CONGRESS ASSEMBLED.

WHEN in the Course of human Events, it becomes necessary for one People to dissolve the Political Bands which have connected them with another, and to assume among the Powers of the Earth, the separate and equal Station to which the Laws of Nature and of Nature's God entitle them, a decent Respect to the Opinions of Mankind requires that they should declare the causes which impel them to the Separation.

Signed by ORDER and in BEHALF of the CONGRESS,

JOHN HANCOCK, PRESIDENT.

ATTEST.
CHARLES THOMSON, SECRETARY.

PHILADELPHIA: PRINTED BY JOHN DUNLAP.

From the very beginning of the colonies' struggle for independence, Hamilton had voiced his ideas. His powerful arguments provided a clear vision for America's future government and laws that would protect citizens' lives and liberty. Some of his ideas are reflected in the Declaration of Independence (*above*), which was signed in 1776.

even those who became revolutionary leaders, were unsure of their right to rebel. Ideas were exchanged through newspapers and pamphlets. Heated arguments occurred in private homes and in public assemblies. When the colonial leaders finally decided to declare independence, they had considered the matter carefully. The nation's founders and the public were convinced by the arguments of men such as Patrick Henry and Alexander Hamilton that they were following the right course. After the revolution, the struggle to decide on the best form of government was approached in the same way.

Alexander Hamilton entered these debates early on. He argued that America had the right to rebel and the potential to become an independent nation. His arguments continued long after the Revolution was won. Hamilton maintained that America needed a strong government and a solid body of laws to protect the life, liberty, and property of its citizens. This was his vision for the United States. Other founders had their own visions for the new nation, and not all of them agreed. Hamilton's arguments prevailed at an important time in America's history, and the result was a prosperous and long-lasting republic.

2. Island Beginnings

One of the most notable aspects of Alexander Hamilton's life is how he rose from unlikely origins to become a great American statesman. Although his policies would help ensure the prosperity of a whole nation, he was born into poverty. He was not born in America, but he dedicated his life to building the United States.

Alexander Hamilton's life began in the Lesser Antilles in the West Indies, a chain of tiny islands that runs from the tip of Puerto Rico to the northeastern coast of South America. In Hamilton's day, the islands of the West Indies were colonies of European powers, such as England and Denmark. A small population of European settlers owned plantations that were worked by multitudes of African slaves. Ships full of trade goods from around the world docked in the port towns to load and to unload their cargoes. People who settled in the West Indies hoped to begin a new life in that lush island paradise and to make a fortune in trade or in agriculture. Some succeeded, but many who came ended up bankrupt.

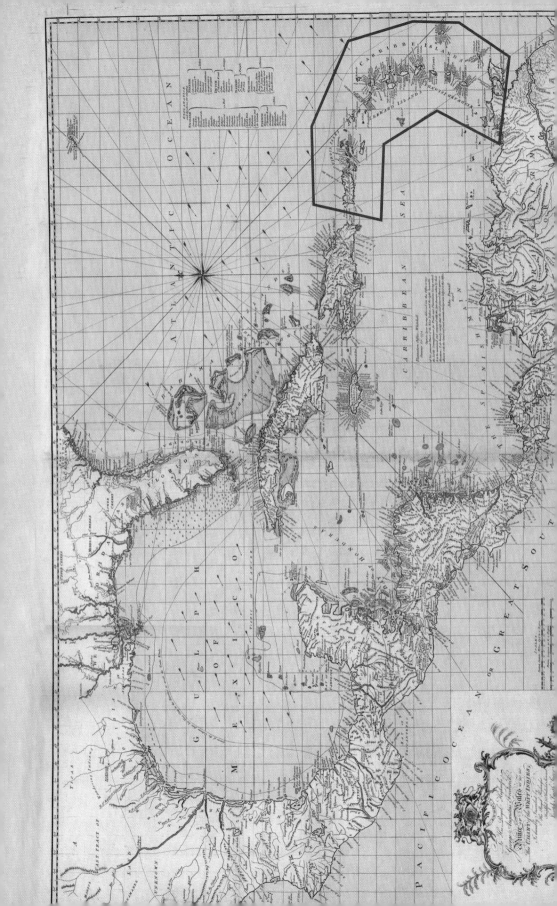

Little is known about Alexander Hamilton's mother, Rachel Fawcett, but it is likely that she was of French descent and had been born and raised on the islands. In 1745, when Rachel was sixteen, she married John Lavien, a planter from the island of Saint Croix. He turned out to be one of the unlucky settlers who did not succeed. His cotton plantation was unprofitable. As his financial circumstances worsened, his marriage to Rachel began to fail. Strong-willed and independent, Rachel refused to remain in that unhappy relationship. Unfortunately the laws at that time were not on Rachel's side. Her attempts to break free from her marriage caused John to have her imprisoned briefly in the city jail in 1750, for being an unruly wife. After her release, Rachel fled from Saint Croix, finally escaping her husband, but also leaving behind their four-year-old son, Peter. When John divorced her several years later, she became legally unable to remarry.

Not long after she left Saint Croix, Rachel took up residence with James Hamilton, a struggling merchant, on the nearby island of Nevis. James seemed a promising partner for Rachel. He was a handsome, charming son of a wealthy Scottish laird, or lord,

---

Opposite: Joseph Smith Speer created this map of the West Indies for George Augustus Frederick, prince of Wales, in 1774. The Lesser Antilles, outlined in red, is where Alexander Hamilton was born. His mother opened a general store in Christiansted where Alexander, then ten years old, learned his first economics lessons.

VIRIDIS ET FRUCTIFERA

Alexʳ Hamilton Esqʳ of Grange Advocate

The Hamilton coat of arms, shown above, illustrates the long Scottish tradition in the family. Notice the oak tree with the saw through it at the top. Legend has it that in 1325, Gilbert de Hamilton challenged John de Spencer to a duel after a disagreement. Spencer refused to fight, but Hamilton killed him anyway and took flight. The angry Spencer family chased him, but Hamilton was able to out-smart the Spencers by switching clothes with some woodcutters.

Alexander Hamilton, after whom James and Rachel would name their youngest son. Although the Hamiltons' landholdings in Scotland were large, James, the fourth son of nine, could not hope to succeed to the lairdship or to inherit much land. He left Scotland for the West Indies to try to make his fortune there.

For nearly ten years, James Hamilton and Rachel Fawcett Lavien lived together, moving from island to island while James pursued his dream of success. Their relationship produced two sons: James, their oldest son, and Alexander, born two years later. To this day, historians are not certain of the year of Alexander Hamilton's

This Georgian-style house is actually a replica of Hamilton's childhood home, which was built in 1680 and was destroyed by a hurricane in the nineteenth century. The building contains memorabilia of his life.

birth. He said he was born in 1757. However, there is evidence in court documents and in Hamilton's early writings that he actually may have been born in 1755.

Unfortunately for Rachel and her new family, James's business ventures were no more successful than were those of John Lavien. Rachel soon found herself in another unhappy situation, raising two sons in near poverty while her irresponsible partner chased his fortune. In 1765, James moved the family from the island of Saint Kitts, where they were then living, to Saint Croix on yet another fruitless business venture. Shortly afterward he returned to Saint Kitts. This time his family did not accompany him. It is not known for sure whether James abandoned his family or whether Rachel, tired of his schemes, refused to go with him. What is clear, however, is that Rachel used the opportunity to take control of her own future. She settled with her boys in the busy port town of Christiansted on Saint Croix and opened a small general store.

Rachel finally found prosperity on her own. Her store, which sold staple items such as flour, rice, and meat, was successful. Of course Rachel was not entirely alone in the enterprise. Alexander, who was nearly ten years old when the store opened, helped his mother by clerking and bookkeeping. The little store in Christiansted was Hamilton's earliest education in economics. He learned about accounting, credit, and creating strong relationships with customers. He also understood the important lesson that the well-being of his family depended on the success of their business. Hamilton would later argue for the United States to be run like a successful business for the sake of national survival.

In 1768, Rachel's newfound freedom and prosperity came to an abrupt end when she became ill and died. Alexander and his brother James were suddenly all alone in the world. To make matters worse, John Lavien filed a lawsuit to claim Rachel's belongings for their son Peter. In court he cruelly declared James and Alexander illegitimate children. They were then unable to inherit anything from their mother's estate. With the swipe of a pen, the Hamilton brothers found themselves penniless.

Their maternal aunt, Ann Lytton, who also lived on Saint Croix, took in Alexander and his brother James. However, the Lyttons were entering into hard financial times of their own, and the boys needed to support themselves. James was apprenticed to a carpenter, while Alexander found fitting employment as a clerk for Nicholas Cruger, who ran an export trading firm in Christiansted. Cruger became a mentor to his young employee, teaching Alexander all he knew about finance and international trade. He entrusted Alexander with adult responsibilities, such as managing the firm's staff and inspecting cargoes.

In his new job, Hamilton came into contact with a great variety of people from all around the world. He also saw the darker side of international trade. Some of

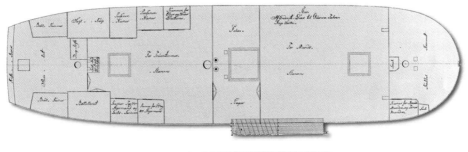

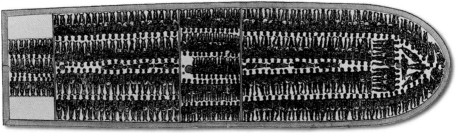

This diagram shows the cramped, wretched conditions on board ships that brought enslaved people across the Atlantic Ocean from Africa. Many Africans died while crossing the ocean. Later in his career, Alexander Hamilton became quite outspoken against slavery. He served as an officer in an antislavery society in New York, and he petitioned the New York legislature to ban the slave trade.

the cargoes he had to inspect were enslaved people recently arrived from Africa. Later in life, he would become outspoken against slavery. In the meantime, everything young Hamilton experienced, both good and bad, became a part of his education.

Another important mentor to Hamilton was the Reverend Hugh Knox, a Presbyterian minister. Knox tutored him in science and in literature. Hamilton read through Knox's library and started writing as well. His poems and articles were occasionally published in the

In Hamilton's earliest known letter, written when he was working for Nicholas Cruger in 1769 to his friend Ned Stevens, Hamilton wished for the event that would change his future. Little did he know at the time that this wish would come true.

". . .my ambition is prevalent that I contemn the grov'ling and condition of a Clerk or the like to which my Fortune condemns me and would willingly risk my life tho' not my Character to exalt my Station. . . . we have seen such Schemes successful when the Projector is Constant I shall conclude saying I wish there was a war."

Here Hamilton explained to Ned that if a person has a goal and works steadily toward it, he will eventually accomplish that goal. However, young Hamilton understood that in his time, war opened up opportunities for disadvantaged but ambitious people like himself. It turned out that the American Revolution provided Hamilton such an opportunity to prove his abilities and to bring him to the attention of great men who would help him "exalt his station," or reach his goal.

local paper. The residents of the island began to take notice of this brilliant young man.

Perhaps the greatest lesson Knox taught Hamilton was the belief that through hard work and willpower people can improve their situations. As a penniless orphan of illegitimate birth, Hamilton might have expected to live out the rest of his life in poverty. Instead he worked toward a better future for himself. His mentors also helped him along. In 1771, Cruger, Knox, and other wealthy islanders raised enough money to send him to America to attend college. Although they hoped that he would study medicine and return to Christiansted to set up a medical practice, Alexander Hamilton never again returned to the islands of his childhood.

3. An American Education

Alexander Hamilton landed at New York Harbor in the autumn of 1772, perhaps carrying a case containing his worldly goods. A young man in his midteens, he was probably dazzled by the bustling city of brownstone buildings and cobblestone streets. It was a contrast to the leisurely pace and breezy, tropical greenery of the Leeward Islands. The population of New York City, some 25,000 people, was larger than that of the whole island of Saint Croix. It appeared that everyone in the city was in a hurry to get somewhere. Even in the mid-eighteenth century, New York City was a businesslike place, where fashionably dressed citizens rushed to and fro on foot, on horseback, and in carriages. New Yorkers already had a reputation for loud talking and fast living. As Hamilton surveyed the hectic city scene from the harbor, he must have liked what he saw. He later chose to settle in New York City.

Next spread: When Alexander Hamilton arrived in New York City, it was a busy center of trade. Many boats entered and exited the harbor. This hand-colored engraving shows the bustling New York Harbor in 1772, the year Hamilton arrived.

NEW YORK, with the ENT

On the day he stepped off the ship, he did not linger in the city. Hamilton's first American destination was Elizabethtown, New Jersey, where he lived with friend Hugh Knox. For a time, he stayed in the elegant manor house of the wealthy Livingston family. Elias Boudinot, a prominent attorney, also welcomed Hamilton into his home. Boudinot and Hamilton remained lifelong friends. The stately mansions and the luxuriant lifestyles of his hosts were another new experience for the boy who grew up in poverty and who never had a stable home.

Hamilton lived with these families while he caught up on his academics. Although he was worldly and gifted, his education had been patchy. To qualify for college entrance, he needed to have some sort of formal

ORTH and EAST RIVERS.

schooling. Therefore, he attended a preparatory academy to round out his education. Hamilton took his studies seriously, and he often brought his books to a nearby cemetery where he could recite his lessons undisturbed.

He finished the academy's program within a year and looked for a college. At first he applied to the College of New Jersey (today's Princeton University). He was turned down, because he wished to complete his studies at his own, quickened pace. Eager to complete his education and to find his way in this exciting new world, Hamilton headed back to New York City to attend King's College (today's Columbia University), which agreed to accept him on his own terms.

Hamilton began his studies at King's College in the fall of 1773. His choice of studies in math, Latin, and

Hamilton attended King's College, today's Columbia University. King's College, on the horizon in this 1763 engraving drawn by Captain Thomas Howdell and engraved by P. Canot, was founded in 1754 with just ten students. The first classes were held in a school-house next to Trinity Church at Broadway and Wall Street.

anatomy revealed his interest in medicine. At the same time, he sharpened his writing and speaking skills. He and a small group of students formed a literary and debating club that met faithfully every week. Hamilton eagerly read modern political philosophy. His favorites were the works of French and Scottish Enlightenment philosophers, such as Charles Montesquieu and John Locke, who challenged traditional views of government. Montesquieu developed the theory of separation of powers to prevent corruption in government. Locke declared that government was a contract between ruler and people that could be broken if the government failed to protect the rights of its citizens. These were revolutionary ideas at a time when a king was believed to rule by divine right. They were also the new philosophies that persuaded the American colonists to break from their king.

Hamilton's interest in debate and politics was strengthened by the historical events unfolding rapidly around him. At the time he first stepped onto the American shore, the colonies were involved in a political upheaval that would soon change the world. The colonists deepened their resistance to England's enforcement of direct taxes. On December 16, 1773, a band of patriots in Boston dumped 342 crates of tea from a ship into the harbor to protest the tax on tea. The Boston Tea Party, as the

This 1789 engraving entitled *Boston Tea Party*,
by W. D. Cooper, captures the fateful event that happened
on December 16, 1773, in response to a tax placed on tea.
Hamilton was in college at the time. His interest in debate and
politics continued to grow as the colonies moved toward rebellion.

The Boston Tea Party set off a string of events that started the American Revolution. To better govern the increasingly disobedient Massachusetts colonists, Parliament passed several acts, called the Intolerable Acts by the colonists, in March 1774. These acts included the closing of the port of Boston and the housing of British troops in vacant buildings. In response, the colonies created the First Continental Congress to demand the repeal of these acts and threaten a boycott of British goods. The British army then marched into Concord, Massachusetts, to seize revolutionaries and their arms. Warned by Paul Revere of the British approach, about seventy minutemen assembled and fired on the seven hundred British troops at Lexington in an attempt to stop their advance on April 19, 1775. The minutemen at Lexington retreated eventually, but the British were met at Concord by nearly four hundred patriot troops. Although the British succeeded in destroying some military supplies, the patriots fired until the British began to retreat back to Boston. Patriots then pursued the tired British troops, firing from behind fences, trees, and buildings. The British suffered around 270 casualties.

protest was called, seemed an expensive but harmless prank, but its boldness shocked the colonies as well as England. The British closed Boston Harbor and increased its military presence in the colonies. After much debate, the colonial assemblies united in support of the Massachusetts rebels. War loomed on the horizon, and Americans realized that they had to choose sides if they had not done so already. Should they be patriots and support independence or should they remain loyal to England and be considered loyalists, or Tories?

During Alexander Hamilton's short stay in America, he had been exposed to both points of view. In New York, Hamilton was surrounded by loyalists. New York had a large Tory population,

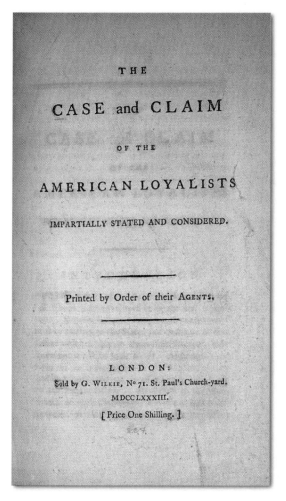

THE

CASE and CLAIM

OF THE

AMERICAN LOYALISTS

IMPARTIALLY STATED AND CONSIDERED.

Printed by Order of their AGENTS,

LONDON:
Sold by G. WILKIE, No 71. St. Paul's Church-yard.
MDCCLXXXIII.
[Price One Shilling.]

The Case and Claim of the American Loyalists Impartially Stated and Considered states the feelings of the loyalists that their rights have been taken away, because they chose to remain loyal to the king.

because its many businessmen feared the rebellion would interfere with trade and profits. In addition, New York politics were controlled by a handful of wealthy families who were fearful of losing their power. Hamilton's own college was known for its loyalism, because its president, Dr. Myles Cooper, supported the Crown and often spoke out against the rebellion.

Despite all of these influences, Hamilton's introduction to American politics was proliberty. His friends in New Jersey, William Livingston and Elias Boudinot, were outspoken in their support of independence. Both took leading roles in the American Revolution. Hamilton was deeply affected by the opinions voiced in those households. He was also influenced by the Enlightenment philosophies he read. He quickly became an enthusiastic supporter of American independence.

In the summer of 1774, the First Continental Congress passed the Non-Importation Act, prohibiting the purchase and the use of goods from England. If all the American colonies agreed to it, England's economy would be damaged. There also was support in Congress to raise local militias to counter the British military occupation.

The acts of Congress sparked a war of words in the colonies. Pamphlets and newspapers rang with fiery arguments for and against these acts. A leading New York Tory named Samuel Seabury, writing under the pen name A Westchester Farmer, published a series of newspaper editorials against the acts of Congress. He

Though Samuel Seabury, in this engraving by T. S. Duche, called himself a farmer in his pamphlets, he was a clergyman and a loyalist.

Hamilton's first political opponent, Samuel Seabury, signed his pamphlets A Westchester Farmer, *but he was not really a farmer. He was an Anglican minister from Westchester County in New York. Although Seabury supported England during the war, he became the first bishop of the Episcopal Church in the United States after the war.*

In his responses to Seabury, Hamilton also used a pen name, A Friend to America. *Many tried to guess which New York politician had penned the well-written pamphlets. Some thought it was John Jay. Myles Cooper, the president of King's College, refused to believe that his young student Hamilton was responsible for those proliberty pamphlets.*

claimed that the Non-Importation Act would benefit merchants and harm farmers. He urged New Yorkers not to obey the acts of Congress, because the acts were treasonous. From his college room, Hamilton made his public debut as a political persuader. In response to Seabury, he wrote two pamphlets encouraging New Yorkers to support Congress and the Non-Importation Act. He argued that Parliament would only respond to financial pressure. He urged New Yorkers to stand united with the other colonies: "If you join with the rest of America in the same common measure, you will be sure to preserve your liberties inviolate."

In his pamphlets, Hamilton made arguments that he would repeat in later years. He would find himself at the center of a bitter conflict between the farmers and the growing merchant class. Unity among the colonies would also reappear as a matter of debate. Unlike some others, Hamilton was able to envision a united America. He was a recent immigrant and was not loyal to any particular colony. He saw that the colonies could benefit by combining under a central government with common interests in mind. However, many outspoken politicians like Seabury cared more about their own interests rather than strengthening America. Hamilton would fight these opinions throughout his career.

As the arguments on paper grew more heated, disturbances in the streets grew as well. Mobs of patriots began using violence against loyalists. Oftentimes these anti-Tory gangs would capture prominent loyalists and jail them, or worse, tar and feather them. Such a mob stormed King's College in November 1775, to tar and feather Myles Cooper. Although Hamilton supported the independence movement, he hated unruly mobs. He raced to the scene and angrily scolded the mob for bringing disgrace to the cause of liberty. Hamilton's speech created a delay that allowed Dr. Cooper to escape. Even though Hamilton and Cooper disagreed about the American Revolution, Hamilton did not want to see his college president fall victim to a mob.

Hamilton's college career ended at around the same time as Cooper's escape. The battles of Lexington, Concord, and Bunker Hill a few months earlier helped convince colonists that the time for arguing was finished. Only war would settle their differences with England. For the past year, Hamilton had been drilling with a militia company to be ready for war. When the war did come, he was appointed captain of artillery for the New York provincial army in March 1776. Hamilton had traded scholarship for arms.

4. Fighting for Independence

As captain of the New York artillery, Hamilton first set out to recruit additional soldiers for his company. He spent the last of his college funds to buy his men the best uniforms and equipment. He trained his company in the complicated process of positioning, loading, and firing cannons. By the time the war reached New York, his artillery company was ready for action.

After driving the British fleet away from Boston Harbor in March 1776, General George Washington and the Continental army hurried to New York where the British fleet was then headed. Upon the general's arrival, Hamilton's company was placed under the command of Henry Knox, Washington's commander of artillery. Hamilton and his men fought with the Continental army during the disastrous battles for New York that followed.

Oppposite: John Trumbull painted George Washington in his military uniform in this 1790 portrait entitled *Washington at Verplanck's Point.* This is how Washington would have looked while Hamilton was his aide-de-camp.

Hamilton's artillery company was placed under the command of General Henry Knox, pictured above in a 1783 portrait by Charles Willson Peale. Under Knox's command, Hamilton's company played a key role in both the Battle of Trenton and the Battle of Princeton.

The British army, under General William Howe, was twice the size of Washington's when it landed in New York. Washington and his small, poorly equipped force desperately tried to hold on to Manhattan Island, but the British had the advantage of a navy and well-trained troops. After a series of defeats, the last rebel fort on Manhattan Island fell to the British in November 1776. The American forces fled to New Jersey and the British occupied New York City.

The loss of New York was a terrible disappointment to the army and to the colonists. Washington needed a victory to keep the cause of independence alive. On Christmas night, Washington and his troops crossed the Delaware River and marched through the night to attack a Hessian outpost in Trenton, New Jersey, at dawn. The attack caught the highly trained German troops, or Hessians, by surprise. Washington and his men captured the entire outpost. A week later, Washington led a similar attack on Princeton, winning another battle. This time he overcame British regular troops. The country rejoiced, and the army was encouraged.

Hamilton's artillery company played a key role in both battles. During these actions, he stood out as a brave and capable officer. Washington had taken notice

Following Spread: This famous 1851 painting by Emanuel Gottlieb Leutze shows Washington crossing the Delaware River on Christmas night in 1776. Washington and his men captured the entire Trenton, New Jersey, outpost. Alexander Hamilton and his artillery company took part in the battle.

When Hamilton was an aide-de-camp for General Washington, he probably had a field desk made of wood and brass. This portable desk held pens, ink, and paper. When it was open it offered a flat place to write letters and orders. This particular desk was used by another patriot, Benjamin Franklin.

and asked Hamilton to become his assistant, or aide-de-camp, as officers' assistants are called in the military. Although Hamilton would have preferred to keep his battlefield command, his artillery company had nearly disappeared due to desertion and illness. As an aide-de-camp, he would be promoted to lieutenant colonel. Most important, he would serve directly under General Washington at his headquarters. He accepted Washington's invitation and received his new rank on March 1, 1777.

General George Washington employed as many as six aides-de-camp at a time. Some were riding aides who delivered messages on horseback. Others were writing aides who did paperwork. Hamilton was a writing aide. He spent long hours writing letters and orders for Washington's signature. He did see action once in a while, however. He came under British fire during a scouting mission outside of Philadelphia, in 1777, and he rode with Washington at the Battle of Monmouth the following year.

This sketch of Martha Washington was done by Colonel Alexander Hamilton. The date is unknown but it is likely he drew it while an aide to Washington.

Washington called his headquarters staff his family. Hamilton developed many close friendships there. Marquis de Lafayette became Hamilton's good friend. Lafayette was a nineteen-year-old French nobleman who sailed to America against his family's wishes to fight for liberty. Colonel John Laurens, a wealthy planter's son from South Carolina, was Hamilton's best friend. They tried unsuccessfully to convince Congress to create a regiment of slaves who would be freed for their service in the army. Their friendship lasted until Laurens was killed in a skirmish in 1782.

Frenchman Marquis de Lafayette, pictured in this portrait painted by Francesco-Giuseppe Casanova between 1781 and 1785, bought a ship when he was nineteen so that he could sail to America and help in its fight for independence. He became a close friend of Hamilton's. Lafayette said that Hamilton possessed a "quickness of perception that is by no means common." Lafayette would later fight for liberty in his own country during the French Revolution.

Hamilton's most important wartime friendship was with George Washington. The working relationship they began at headquarters lasted for more than twenty years. Washington developed a deep regard for Hamilton's abilities and ideas. The general chose Hamilton to conduct his most important business, such as prisoner exchanges with the British. Hamilton also was fluent in French and was popular with the Europeans at headquarters. Consequently he became a liaison to the French commanders when their country joined the American cause. Washington's trust in Hamilton can be seen in the general's letter to the French admiral, the Comte d'Estaing. Washington introduced Hamilton as someone "in whom I place entire confidence. He will be able to make you perfectly acquainted with my sentiments . . . consider the information he delivers as coming from myself."

As the war progressed, the situation at headquarters became gloomy. At the end of 1777, Washington had lost Philadelphia to the British while his rival general, Horatio Gates, won a stunning victory at Saratoga, New York. Winter camp at Valley Forge, Pennsylvania, from 1777 to 1778, brought new problems on the political front. Washington constantly had to beg Congress for food and clothing for his nine thousand cold, hungry men. Under the Articles of Confederation, the American constitution at that time, Congress had no authority to impose war taxes. Congress could only ask the states to contribute, and the states normally refused. Congress had to advise Washington to scavenge the countryside for supplies. Hamilton wrote much of the correspondence with Congress and shared Washington's frustration. The states were starving their own army in the field while expecting to win a war against the greatest military power on the globe!

Hamilton's experience at Valley Forge shaped his thoughts about the new nation. It angered him that Congress's weakness endangered the cause of liberty and the future of America. Hamilton also looked beyond the borders of America. He feared that the government would appear foolish to foreign nations, such as France, which supported the American cause. "How can we hope for success in our European negotiations if [they] have no confidence in the wisdom . . . of the great Continental Government?" he asked in a letter to the governor of New York.

At least America's military situation began to improve in 1778. Washington battled the British successfully in Monmouth, New Jersey, in June. The French entered the war that summer, raising hopes in America and putting pressure on the British to end the war. England then had to stretch its military power to fight two enemies.

Late in 1780, Hamilton became unhappy at headquarters. He was tired of sitting at a desk and wanted to return to the action of the battlefield. He had asked Washington on several occasions for a field command

Cornwallis's surrender at Yorktown is shown in the engraving from the late 1700s or early 1800s. It is based on a painting by John Trumbull. Washington is depicted here with his officers. Hamilton is the first of the three standing soldiers, from the left, Hamilton's friend John Laurens is beside him.

that would, in his words, "raise my character as a soldier above mediocrity." Washington refused, because Hamilton was too valuable to him as an aide. In February 1781, Hamilton used a small quarrel with Washington as an excuse to quit headquarters. Washington called him back in July of that year with the chance for military glory that Hamilton had wanted. Washington gave Hamilton command of a regiment and orders to help lead an attack on the British at Yorktown, Virginia. The attack began on October 14,

1781. Cornered by American forces on land and the French fleet at sea, British general Charles Cornwallis surrendered. Hamilton, Lafayette, and Laurens, who all had commands in the battle, proudly attended the surrender ceremony that followed. After many uncertain years of struggle, American independence had been won.

In the end, the war in North America had become too costly for the British. The entry of France, and then Spain in 1779, in the conflict strained British forces and the British treasury to the point of breaking. The war had become unpopular in England, and there was a great outcry to end it. These reasons all contributed to the decision of King George III to let his former colonies go.

Until the final peace treaty was signed on November 30, 1783, American and French forces remained on duty. Hamilton, however, had earned his military reputation and wanted to move on with his life. He resigned from the army on March 1, 1782.

5. Peacetime Pursuits

Alexander Hamilton was only in his midtwenties when he left the military, but he had already set the foundation for his postwar life. While at headquarters, he had become a politician. He had also found a wife and started a family during his time there.

During the frequent lulls in fighting, especially during wintertime, Washington's headquarters became the center of a lively social scene. Washington and his staff often entertained visitors with dinners and dances. The visitors included plenty of young ladies, and the staff officers competed good-naturedly for their attention. Hamilton had been very popular with the ladies. Although he was often described as small and frail, he really was of average height for his day, 5' 7" (1.7 m) tall, and very thin. His grandson described him as "uncommonly handsome" with blond hair, violet eyes,

---

Next page: This portrait by James Sharples was the Hamilton family's favorite portrait of Alexander Hamilton. Here Hamilton is in his midtwenties. He wears his hair in the popular style of his time, long and tied with a ribbon in a ponytail. Men did not wear wigs at that time, but they powdered their hair so that it would be scented and colored a dignified gray.

This engraving by D. Huntington, believed to have been created in 1789, shows a reception held by Martha Washington. George and Martha Washington were known for their entertaining, both during the war and later during Washington's presidency. They chose to entertain in formal style, deliberately emphasizing the new republic's wish to be accepted as the equal of the established governments of Europe.

and rosy cheeks. His bearing was usually dignified, but he was witty and quick to laugh, especially in the company of ladies. Hamilton soon fell in love with Elizabeth Schuyler, one of the women who often visited headquarters. Hamilton and Schuyler were married on December 14, 1780.

Elizabeth, or Betsey as Hamilton called her, was the second daughter of Philip Schuyler, a major general in the army. Schuyler was also a wealthy landowner and a politician from New York state. Hamilton, a penniless

Elizabeth Schuyler Hamilton, or Betsey, was very close to her husband. Shown here as she looked in 1787, Betsey was described by one of Hamilton's friends as having "the most dark, lovely eyes that I ever saw." This portrait was painted by Ralph Earl while he was in prison for debt. Betsey Hamilton agreed to sit for Earl to help raise money for his release.

immigrant, was an unlikely match for a woman like Betsey. Schuyler, like many officers in Washington's army, thought highly of Hamilton, though. He was delighted with the match.

Betsey was twenty-three when she married Hamilton. While her husband worked tirelessly for the country, she ably managed their household. Hamilton often asked her for her opinions on his writings and speeches. Betsey and Hamilton remained devoted to each other until Hamilton's death, twenty-four years later. They had nine children in all, seven sons and two daughters.

Hamilton used his spare time at headquarters to communicate with prominent statesmen. He did an enormous amount of planning on how to improve the government. He was confident and outspoken in his opinions. In 1780, Hamilton had written to a New York congressman about his "ideas of the defects of our present system [of government] and the changes necessary to save us from ruin." The defect, or problem, was the inability of Congress to raise money through taxes. The states resisted the suggestion of a national tax on imports. Import taxes were a large source of revenue for governments. However, the individual states held the right to tax imports and did not want to share that power with Congress. As a result, the army was unpaid, national debts mounted, and America slid into bankruptcy.

In 1781, Hamilton made his opinions public in six essays he titled "The Continentalist." He argued that the foundation of a strong, respectable nation was a sound economy. He pleaded for Congress to be given more authority over the states. The "want of power in Congress," he stated, was the source of many "fatal mistakes, which have so deeply endangered the common cause." While Congress remained unable to pay its debts, Hamilton warned, America would "neither have dignity, vigor, nor credit." These three principles were essential to Hamilton's ideal government: Dignity among the nations of the world; vigor, or energy, so that the government could act quickly in times of need; and credit to enable borrowing and to attract investors.

"The Continentalist" brought Hamilton to the attention of America's most powerful politicians. Robert Morris, superintendent of finance in Congress, was one of them. Morris appointed Hamilton continental receiver of taxes for the state of New York in 1782. In that job, Hamilton found out firsthand how difficult it was to collect money for Congress. He collected more excuses than money! The experience strengthened his opinion that Congress needed more power.

In July of that year, he was appointed New York's delegate to the Continental Congress. He endured more disappointments there. The states still refused to approve a national import tax. The tax was needed to pay the army, which at that time was still in the field. While Congress debated, the army rebelled. In June 1783, hundreds of unpaid soldiers marched to

Philadelphia to protest directly to Congress. Congress handled the situation by fleeing to Princeton, New Jersey. Frustrated, Hamilton submitted a proposal calling for a national convention to improve the government, but it was ignored. When his term ended in July 1783, Hamilton left Congress in disgust.

Leaving politics behind, Hamilton established a law practice. He had earned his law degree shortly after he left the army in 1782. After his Congressional term, he moved his family, which now included a baby son, Philip, to New York City. He rented an apartment at 57 Wall Street and opened a law office next door. He was soon busy defending former loyalists against the Trespass Act. Passed in New York in 1783, the act allowed patriots who had fled the city during the war to sue Tories who had occupied their property. Although defending loyalists was unpopular, Hamilton chose principle over popularity. The Trespass Act cases enabled him to promote his vision for the country.

He was concerned about America's foreign relations. The Treaty of Paris in 1783, which ended the American Revolution, included a promise that the United States would not punish former British loyalists. The Trespass Act violated the treaty. Hamilton argued in court that states' laws could not overrule international treaties. One case, *Rutgers v. Waddington*, made national headlines. Although Hamilton did not win the case, his forceful arguments caused the jury to award only minimal

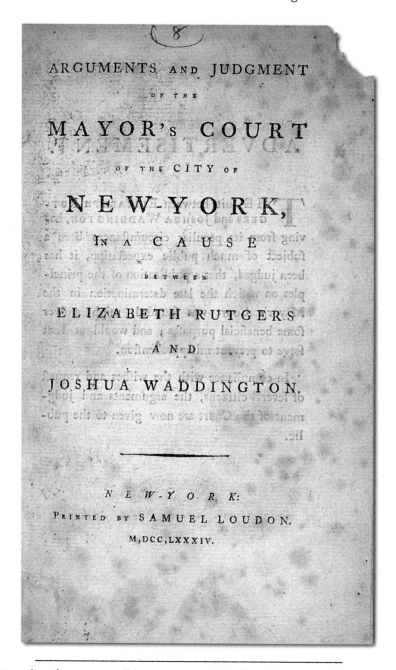

ARGUMENTS AND JUDGMENT

OF THE

MAYOR's COURT

OF THE CITY OF

NEW-YORK,

IN A CAUSE

BETWEEN

ELIZABETH RUTGERS

AND

JOSHUA WADDINGTON.

NEW-YORK:

PRINTED BY SAMUEL LOUDON.

M,DCC,LXXXIV.

Hamilton became well known as a defender of loyalists after the American Revolution ended. One of his most famous cases was *Rutgers v. Waddington*. In 1783, New York passed the Trespass Act, which allowed patriots to sue for damages against loyalists who had occupied their homes during the war. Hamilton believed the Trespass Act violated the Treaty of Paris. The courts agreed, and the law was overturned.

damages against the Tory defendant. Opponents of Hamilton's position felt the judgment endangered individual liberties by limiting the powers of the states.

Hamilton, as usual, was looking into the future. He argued that, instead of "laboring to . . . punish Tories and explain away treaties," America needed to improve its reputation abroad. America had joined the independent nations of the world, therefore America needed to "act in a manner consistent with the dignity of that station."

Even though Hamilton considered his position a matter of good statesmanship, others became suspicious of him. They only saw that he was taking the Tories' side. Hamilton became a controversial figure in national politics because of the highly publicized *Rutgers v. Waddington* case.

6. Fighting for a New Government

By early 1786, the Hamiltons had two more children, a daughter named Angelica and a son named Alexander. Hamilton concentrated on his law practice and on his growing family. At that time, there were only thirty-five other attorneys practicing in New York. They were a close-knit group that sometimes cocounseled and sometimes opposed each other in the courtroom. Robert Troupe, Hamilton's good friend, opened his law office next door to Hamilton's. Another young, successful attorney in town was Aaron Burr.

Even though he had a large family to support, Hamilton was known for undercharging clients. He often took charity cases for which he received little or no payment. His friends joked that if Hamilton refused to raise his fees, they would have to pay to bury him when he died. Their prediction would turn out to be true.

Other projects kept Hamilton busy during the postwar years. In February 1784, he helped establish the Bank of New York, the state's first bank. He also became active in New York's antislavery movement as a founding member

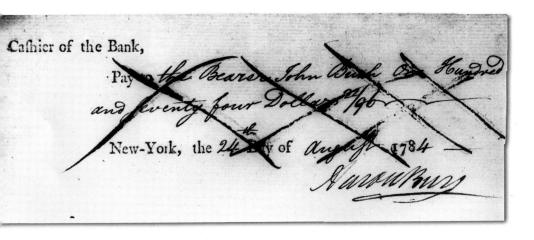

Above is a canceled check from the Bank of New York during the year in which it was established. The check, dated August 24, 1784, was signed by Aaron Burr.

of the Society for Promoting the Manumission of Slaves. The aim of the society, created in 1785, was to ensure that freed slaves were not forced back into slavery. The following year, Hamilton and his associates petitioned the New York assembly to end the slave trade.

In 1786, Hamilton was elected to the New York state assembly. The states were still arguing about trade, and a special convention was called to address the matter. Hamilton was appointed to attend the convention that met in Annapolis, Maryland, in September 1786. Only five states bothered to send delegates, so no official work could be done. Nevertheless those who did meet at

James Madison of Virginia is pictured here in a 1796–1797 painting by James Sharples. Madison and Hamilton worked together to address the problems of a new government.

Annapolis, particularly Hamilton and James Madison of Virginia, used the opportunity to discuss the problems with the government. Hamilton wrote a petition to Congress to sponsor another convention, this time to create an entirely new plan of government. The other delegates supported it.

A disturbance in Massachusetts made Congress take the petition seriously. In 1787, hundreds of armed farmers, under the leadership of Daniel Shays, marched on the state supreme court to protest heavy land taxes. The protest, called Shays's Rebellion, was stopped by military force, but it alarmed the country. Many thought the protests were evidence of the disorder in American politics. Shortly after the rebellion, Congress approved the convention.

New York had become rich and powerful under the Articles of Confederation. The state's most prominent politicians opposed the convention. The most outspoken opponent was Governor George Clinton. Clinton had been one of Hamilton's wartime correspondents, so Clinton knew exactly where the young statesman stood on the issue of national government. The governor had no choice but to send Hamilton, who had drafted the convention proposal, but he also sent two other hand-picked men who opposed the convention. Hamilton's voice was sure to be overruled.

The convention met in Philadelphia during the summer of 1787. Because the future of the nation was

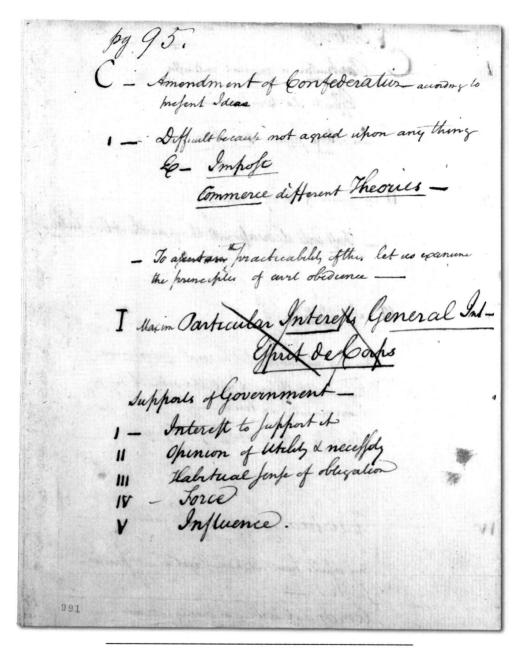

pg 95.

C — Amendment of Confederation according to present Ideas

1 — Difficult because not agreed upon any thing
&— Impost
Commerce different Theories —

— To ascertain the practicability of this let us examine the principles of civil obedience ———

I Maxim Particular Interests General Int—
~~Spirit de Corps~~

Supports of Government —

1 — Interest to support it
II — Opinion of Utility & necessity
III — Habitual sense of obligation
IV — Force
V — Influence.

991

At the 1787 convention in Philadelphia, Hamilton presented a plan that featured centralized power of the government. Pictured above is a page from his convention notes. Alexander Hamilton's speech was one of the longest at the convention. Some historians believe that Hamilton's June 18 speech was his most important public document, because it outlined his philosophy of government.

in the hands of the convention, the states picked their most trusted leaders as delegates. George Washington and Benjamin Franklin were just two of the great men who attended.

The convention spent most of its time debating two plans of government. Virginia, led by James Madison, presented a plan that called for a president, a supreme court, and a two-branch legislature whose membership was based on population. The smaller states felt that the Virginia plan was not fair to them, because the larger states would have more representation in Congress. New Jersey submitted a plan that called for equal representation in the legislature for all states.

Hamilton was the only individual to present a plan. His five- or six-hour speech was the longest of the convention. His plan reflected the strong feelings he had against state sovereignty and in support of centralized power. He reduced the states to simple administrative districts. His plan called for an assembly elected by the people, and a president. The convention audience listened politely, but no vote was taken on his plan. The majority of delegates were opposed to removing state power entirely. Hamilton's idea of a president sounded too much like a king.

After nearly four months of difficult debate, the convention finally decided upon a constitution. The two-house legislature of the Virginia plan was adopted, but with equal representation for each state in the Senate, and a House of Representatives based on state population. A system of checks and balances was created whereby the three branches of the government could not abuse their authority. Hamilton felt that the states still had too much power in the new government. However, he reasoned that the new constitution was at least an improvement on the old system. Other delegates had doubts, too. Hamilton strongly urged them to sign the constitution anyway. He wasn't able to convince his fellow New York delegates, who had left the convention in protest. Hamilton's signature is the only one from New York.

Now the states had to vote on the constitution. Nine of the thirteen states needed to approve, or ratify, the Constitution for it to go into effect. Hamilton hurried back to New York to argue for the Constitution. Because New York was a large and powerful state, its support was necessary to the success of the new government. Unfortunately Governor Clinton had been spending that summer gathering an opposition to whatever came out of Philadelphia. When Hamilton returned, the newspapers were already denouncing the new constitution as a conspiracy to destroy individual liberties. Those who opposed the Constitution were called Anti-Federalists, because they favored state power and did not want the proposed federal government instituted.

As usual Hamilton responded by writing. In October 1787, he began work on a series of essays that he titled "The Federalist." The title reflected the author's support of the proposed federal government. Through this series, Hamilton hoped to gain popular support for the Constitution by explaining it. In the first essay, he appealed to his readers to accept the new government as "the safest course for your liberty, your dignity, and your happiness." Hamilton asked for help on the series from James Madison and New York statesman John Jay. They turned out eighty-five essays in the span of seven months. Hamilton alone wrote at least fifty-one. "The Federalist" was quickly recognized as an authority on the Constitution. The collection of essays have been published in book form, entitled *The Federalist Papers*. They are still read widely and considered a masterpiece of American political thought.

The New York ratifying convention met in Poughkeepsie to debate and to vote on the Constitution. Hamilton and the other supporters of the Constitution were outnumbered two to one. Days of heated,

Hamilton worked with James Madison and John Jay to write *The Federalist Papers*. Jay is pictured here in an 1875 painting believed to be based on a portrait by John Trumbull.

the Emperor.
the King of
ng.
is Papa's let-

ring up Ave
le.
with a paper

ttle money to

g, thinking,
ding.
reatife on the
cific gravity

he Emperor's
Holland.
the comforts
a profperous

r laft.

rrellis; Car-

lburne.
zo Bay, Ja-

s.

phia.
more.

For the Independent Journal.

The FŒDERALIST. No. I.

To the People of the State of New-York.

AFTER an unequivocal experience of the ineffi-
cacy of the fubfifting Fœderal Government, you are
called upon to deliberate on a new Conftitution for
the United States of America. The fubject fpeaks
its own importance; comprehending in its confequen-
ces, nothing lefs than the exiftence of the UNION,
the fafety and welfare of the parts of which it is com-
pofed, the fate of an empire, in many refpects, the
moft interefting in the world. It has been frequent-
ly remarked, that it feems to have been referved to
the people of this country, by their conduct and example, to decide the important queftion, whether fo-
cieties of men are really capable or not, of eftablifh-
ing good government from refection and choice, or
whether they are forever deftined to depend, for their
political conftitutions, on accident and force. If there
be any truth in the remark, the crifis, at which we
are arrived, may with propriety be regarded as the
æra in which that decifion is to be made; and a wrong
election of the part we fhall act, may, in this view,
deferve to be confidered as the general misfortune of
mankind.

This idea will add the inducements of philanthropy
to thofe of patriotifm to heighten the follicitude, which
all confiderate and good men muft feel for the event.
Happy will it be if our choice fhould be decided by a judicious eftimate of our true interefts,
unperplexed and unbiaffed by confiderations not connected with the public good. But this is a thing more
ardently to be wifhed, than ferioufly to be expected.
The plan offered to our deliberations, affects too many particular interefts, innovates upon too many local
inftitutions, not to involve in its difcuffion a variety
of objects foreign to its merits, and of views, paffi-
ons and prejudices little favourable to the difcovery

"The Federalist No. 1" was first printed in the *New-York
Independent Journal* on October 21, 1787. The series of essays
by Hamilton, Madison, and Jay were collected into what is now
called *The Federalist Papers*. These essays explained the Constitution.

and sometimes angry, debate followed, but the Anti-Federalists would not budge. Only when word came that Virginia ratified the Constitution did the Anti-Federalists of New York decide to approve it on July 27, 1788. Soon the United States had a new government. For years Hamilton had argued tirelessly for a stronger government. His power of persuasion and his ability to rally others who held the same ideas were greatly responsible for the creation of the new federal republic.

7. Secretary of the Treasury

The new U.S. government assembled in New York City, the nation's first capital, in April 1789. Newly elected president George Washington's first task was to appoint his cabinet secretaries. The secretaries would be his closest advisers, so he needed the best minds he could find. Thomas Jefferson, who was in Paris as minister to France, agreed to return to America as secretary of state. Washington chose his former artillery general, Henry Knox, to be secretary of war. The president picked another wartime colleague, Alexander Hamilton, to be secretary of the treasury. Both Washington and Hamilton favored a strong federal government, mainly because they had shared the same frustrations during the war. At that time, the treasury position was the most important in the cabinet. The United States was bankrupt, and the success of the new government depended on the treasury

Opposite: George Washington, pictured in this 1796 oil painting by Gilbert Stuart, was the first president of the United States. He chose his cabinet secretaries to steer the new country toward stability and prosperity. A cabinet is a group of advisers that a president appoints to help make decisions. Alexander Hamilton was the first treasury secretary.

With the approval of Congress, three executive departments, headed by secretaries, comprised Washington's cabinet. The secretary of the treasury handled the government's financial affairs. The secretary of state was responsible for advising on foreign affairs. The secretary of war was responsible for administering the armed forces. This position is called the secretary of defense today. The attorney general, the country's top law officer, was also a part of Washington's cabinet.

secretary's ability to rescue the nation's finances.

Hamilton had spent most of his time in America thinking about America's financial problems and how to fix them. His thinking had been greatly influenced by the Scottish philosopher David Hume. In his economic writings of the mid-eighteenth century, Hume discussed how commerce and industry could help developing nations become strong and prosperous. In Hume's day, land was considered the primary form of wealth. Times were changing, however. According to Hume, paper currency was the wealth of the future. Money changed hands easily and funded commerce and industry. Hume also believed that paper wealth was only useful to the community when held in large

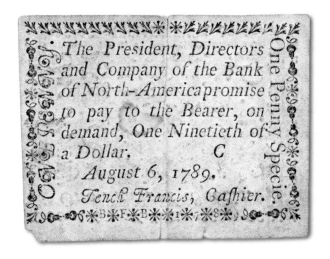

Above is an example of paper currency from 1789. Hamilton was convinced that the use of paper money was critical to the growth and success of the new nation. His beliefs were based on David Hume's philosophical writings. Hamilton presented plans for a national bank as well as a mint that would issue money for the new nation.

sums by businessmen, who could then invest it in beneficial enterprises. Hamilton agreed. He knew that the United States would prosper only if he encouraged the growth of commerce and the business community.

Hume used England's economy as his model; so did Hamilton. England was the wealthiest and the most powerful country in the world. Hamilton believed that the United States could become even more powerful than England. However, the English financial system was controversial in the United States. Hamilton could overlook past disagreements, but many Americans continued to hate England. They thought the English system was corrupt and did not want their new republic to be like their former mother country in any way. Hamilton soon found out that his vision clashed with anti-English opinions. The two opposing viewpoints on the nation's finances created strong political divisions that would later develop into a party system.

Hamilton concentrated first on dealing with the national debt that had been growing since 1776. Congress, various government agencies, and the individual states had all issued securities promising to pay their creditors. The creditors were foreign countries, soldiers, and farmers who had supplied the war effort. Hamilton calculated the national debt at around $54 million, an enormous sum for that time.

Hamilton submitted his financial plan to Congress in a series of famous reports. His first *Report on Public Credit* was turned in on January 14, 1790, five months after he took office. Several more reports would follow. To Congress's surprise, he did not simply offer a scheme to pay off the debt. Rather he created a far-reaching program to restore the credit and the dignity of the nation.

Hamilton's program proposed refunding the debt by offering a trade-in on all the old securities, including those issued by the states, for new interest-bearing federal bonds. The bonds could be bought and traded on

Opposite: Hamilton's plan for the United States was to create a financial empire. He used England's financial system as a model. At the time, England had the most successful economy in the world. Charles Willson Peale painted Hamilton around 1791, at about the same time he published his *Report on Public Credit*.

the market or held as an investment. Funds to pay interest on all of these bonds would come from import and excise taxes. If carried out, Hamilton's plan would create a large base of revenue to enable the government to pay all of its obligations.

Hamilton also proposed a national bank, based on the Bank of England, that could loan and deposit funds for the government as well as for businesses. The bank notes would circulate like paper money. Another part of his plan called for Congress to promote manufacturing so the United States would need fewer imported goods. Hamilton hoped industry would help create a diverse workforce. Laborers as well as farmers would be able to make a good living in America.

Hamilton's design was to turn the United States eventually into a commercial empire. Not everyone liked the plan, though. Southerners in the government objected to it, particularly Virginians such as James Madison, who was a member of the House of Representatives, and Secretary of State Thomas Jefferson. Although these men had worked together to unite the country, they had different visions of what kind of country it should be. Jefferson and Madison, both plantation owners, pictured America as a republic of farmers who grew their own food and made their own clothes. They feared that commerce and industry would lead to the growth of cities and would ruin the character of the country. Jefferson and Madison were

Plantation owners did not agree with Hamilton's plan. They were concerned that a focus on commerce would harm the new nation's character. The economy of the southern states revolved around agriculture and plantations, like the one pictured in this 1790 engraving. Hamilton's plan called for greater industrialization.

also among those who strongly disliked the similarities to the English system in Hamilton's plan.

The Virginians and their supporters had other reasons for opposing the funding plan. Desperate for cash, many farmers and soldiers, mainly from the southern states, had sold their wartime securities to speculators at reduced prices. The speculators were mostly wealthy, northern businessmen who gambled that the American government would eventually pay on the securities. The proposed payout would put a great deal of wealth into those few hands. The Virginians objected strongly to the federal assumption of state debts. Virginia had paid nearly its entire war debt, whereas northern states, such as Massachusetts, had paid next to nothing. Many southerners complained that Hamilton's plan favored businessmen over landholders and the northern states over the southern states.

As an alternative, Madison proposed dividing the value of the new federal bonds between the original and the current holders. This plan would spread around the wealth. He also called for the government to reimburse the states that had already paid their debts in addition to assuming the existing debts.

Unlike men such as Madison, Hamilton was thinking about the long term. He argued that it would be a grave breach of trust to cheat investors of their expected payment. If they did, U.S. bonds thereafter would be considered a bad risk, and no one would want to invest in them. The nation's credit would be ruined before it was established. The concentration of wealth helped Hamilton's plan, too. The businessmen who profited most would hopefully invest their money back into the nation. As far as reimbursing debt-free states, Hamilton objected that such a move would double the federal government's current debt.

Congress debated Hamilton's plan fiercely and nearly rejected it. Hamilton tried to rally the support of congressmen. One senator observed that Hamilton "spends most of his time running from place to place among the Members [of Congress]." Hamilton finally asked Thomas Jefferson for help. According to Jefferson, Hamilton was "dejected beyond description," his appearance "neglected" from worry about the failure of his plan. Jefferson wrote a famous account of the deal they finally struck. Jefferson invited Hamilton and James Madison to dinner to work out a compromise. The three of them decided that Madison would not fight the assumption plan in Congress if Hamilton and his supporters agreed to a southern location for the permanent national capital. The deal worked. Hamilton's plan was approved along with a bill to move the capital to a location on the Potomac River, today's Washington, D.C. A temporary location at Philadelphia was chosen to satisfy the middle states' delegates.

However, Jefferson would not make a deal in favor of the national bank plan. The proposed bank was modeled after the Bank of England. In Jefferson's view, the Bank of England was a corrupt institution that provided government money to wealthy businessmen. Jefferson had regional concerns in mind as well. The bank would only benefit paper money holders, mostly northern businessmen. Southern planters bartered goods, and their wealth was mainly land.

In their struggle for the bank, Hamilton and Jefferson disagreed on how the Constitution should be interpreted. Jefferson claimed that because the Constitution did not specifically give Congress the power to create a bank, a national bank was unconstitutional. Jefferson's view, which sought to limit the powers of the federal government, is called strict constructionism. Washington nearly accepted Jefferson's argument but first asked Hamilton for his opinion. Hamilton responded with a written defense entitled "Opinion on the Constitutionality of a National Bank." Hamilton pointed out that the Constitution allows Congress to "make all laws that are necessary and proper" for the public good. This means that Congress can act for the benefit of the country even if the action is not specified in the Constitution. Therefore the creation of a national bank was a constitutional means to help establish public credit. His argument was the first use of the implied powers doctrine. Washington considered both sides carefully and finally agreed with Hamilton. The president signed the bank bill into law on February 25, 1796.

Just as Hamilton had envisioned, the country prospered under his system. Federal import duties and excise taxes provided a solid base of revenue. Government bonds offered on the market sold out within a few weeks. Stock exchanges sprang up in New York and in Philadelphia to support the brisk trade. News of Hamilton's funding scheme reached across the Atlantic Ocean, and Europeans invested millions in the American economy. In spite of Hamilton's success, opposition continued to form against him.

8. Struggle in the Cabinet

Thomas Jefferson was deeply troubled by the passage of the bank bill. He felt that the government was being given too much power. He also believed that Hamilton was becoming too powerful. Hamilton and his supporters were known as Federalists, because they backed a strong federal government. Jefferson, Madison, and their supporters created their own party. They called themselves Republicans, because they claimed to uphold republican principles. They found allies among Hamilton's old Anti-Federalist rivals in New York, including Aaron Burr. Burr had recently ousted Hamilton's father-in-law from his Senate seat and seemed eager to chip away at Hamilton's power.

When Congress convened in Philadelphia in 1791, both sides went to war in the press. As secretary of the treasury, Hamilton had kept his habit of publishing articles in the press to gain support for his opinions. Jefferson struck back by starting a Republican newspaper. He encouraged James Madison to write for the paper, because he believed that Madison was the only

Charles Willson Peale painted this portrait of Thomas Jefferson in 1791 while Jefferson was secretary of state. Jefferson thought Hamilton's ideas about the U.S. government would create an elite ruling class similar to the one found in England. Jefferson would later become the third president of the United States.

match for Hamilton. "You must, my dear Sir, take up your pen against this champion!" Jefferson wrote to him on one occasion. Republicans denounced the Federalists for being pro-British and for creating a rich ruling class through their financial policies. The Federalist press responded by claiming that Republicans were trying to destroy the government that they worked so hard to create. The tone of the articles in the papers became more shrill and bitter as time went on.

George Washington was painfully aware of the newspaper war. He tried his best to end the conflict. The president wrote to Hamilton and to Jefferson, pleading with them to end the "wounding suspicions, and irritating charges" in the newspapers. Washington worried that the new political divisions would tear apart the nation. He admitted to Hamilton in a letter, "I do not see how the Reins of Government are to be managed, or how the Union of the States can be much longer preserved."

Like bickering brothers, Hamilton and Jefferson each denied any wrongdoing. Each believed that he represented the true interests of the country. Meanwhile the newspaper war continued. Washington was so troubled by these events that he nearly retired at the end of his first term. Hamilton and Jefferson both urged him to run for reelection, and Washington reluctantly agreed. However, his secretaries did not stop fighting. Shortly after Washington was reelected in December 1792, Jefferson tried to have Hamilton thrown out of office on

Gazette of the United States was the newspaper that Hamilton used to publish his articles promoting the Federalist cause. Above is the issue published on Wednesday, April 15, 1789.

corruption charges brought before the House of Representatives. No proof was found, and the charges were thrown out instead.

Hamilton and Jefferson then began to clash about foreign relations. Hamilton supported better relations with England, because it was the most powerful and stable European nation. A strong trade partnership with England was important to his financial program. Jefferson still considered England an enemy and favored strong ties with France, America's wartime ally. For many years ahead, the United States would desperately try to avoid war with both England and France.

In 1789, the French people had followed the Americans' example and rebelled against their king. However, France's revolution turned into a bloodbath in the span of a few years. At the outset, some French people favored keeping their king along with a constitution that ensured the rights of all people. A more extreme faction, called the Jacobins, wanted to do away with the king altogether and create a republic. In January 1793, the Jacobins gained power, and King Louis XVI was beheaded, along with Queen Marie-Antoinette. The Jacobins followed this event with the bloody Reign of Terror. Tens of thousands of people who opposed the Jacobins were sent to the guillotine. Thousands more were imprisoned. Most Americans celebrated France's revolution, but Hamilton and others, including Washington, were horrified by its brutality. To make matters worse, France declared war against England. The United States was in danger of being drawn into the war because of an alliance with France that was signed during the American Revolution.

Hamilton knew that another war with England would ruin America's financial recovery. He therefore advised Washington to declare neutrality and to suspend the alliance with France. Hamilton argued that treaties are made between governments, not countries. The United States had signed the treaty with the king of France. Because the king of France had been killed and the government of that country had changed, Hamilton reasoned that the United States no longer had to abide by the treaty.

Jefferson, on the other hand, supported the French Revolution. Despite the violence, he believed order would be restored and liberty would be won. Jefferson recommended keeping the alliance while maintaining a friendly neutrality. Jefferson's opinion prevailed until the French ambassador Edmund Genêt violated the neutrality by directing military operations against England from his post in America. Jefferson finally agreed to request Genêt's recall, ending diplomatic ties to revolutionary France. This was one of Jefferson's last acts of office. He resigned as secretary of state on December 31, 1793.

America's neutrality and Genêt's actions angered the British. The British navy began capturing American ships sailing in French territories. Congress considered a trade embargo with England, and war was possible. With Jefferson gone, Hamilton was Washington's top adviser for foreign policy. He recommended a peace mission to England to prevent a costly war. Washington agreed and sent Chief Justice John Jay to London to work out a peace treaty.

Soon afterward, in January 1795, Hamilton resigned his post at the Department of the Treasury. However, he continued to advise Washington on matters of policy, and he remained active in the ongoing newspaper war defending Federalist policies. When John Jay's treaty with England turned out to be unpopular, Hamilton helped avoid war with England once again with his skillful arguments in support of the treaty.

At the end of his second term, Washington had had enough of politics and did not run again. The elections of 1796 brought John Adams into the presidency, and Thomas Jefferson was elected vice president. Adams kept Washington's cabinet ministers, who, like their former chief, asked Hamilton for advice. A war crisis with France was looming because of the Jay Treaty. Without Adams's knowledge, Hamilton worked with Secretary of War James McHenry and Secretary of State Timothy Pickering to send a peace mission to France in 1797. However, the French ministry demanded $250,000 from the peace commission before they would talk. News of this bribery attempt, called the XYZ Affair after the code letters given to the three commissioners, enraged

This illustration shows a doll representing John Jay being burned in response to the treaty he negotiated with England in 1794. This was a common way to protest unpopular political acts.

America. There was a great outcry from Americans for war preparations to be made against France.

John Adams called George Washington out of retirement to command the army in 1798. Washington promptly appointed Hamilton second in command. Hamilton's love of military duty was rekindled, and he donned his general's uniform eagerly. He did not want to rush into a declaration of war, but he believed that hostilities were unavoidable at that point and wanted the country to be prepared. He not only readied the army for war but also began creating a long-term plan for the military. In the meantime, Adams had second thoughts and decided to send another peace mission to France. Because the majority of Federalists supported war, many in the party felt that Adams had betrayed them.

This political cartoon about the XYZ Affair shows a five-headed monster that represents Paris. In the cartoon, Americans, called X, Y, and Z, resist threats and demands for money from revolutionary France. The United States's 1797 peace mission to France was interrupted by a bribery attempt, and war with France seemed possible.

In addition, Adams had found out about Hamilton's involvement in his cabinet and dismissed McHenry and Pickering. The president made no secret that he disliked Hamilton because of his low birth and youthful ambition. When Washington died at Mount Vernon in the middle of the war crisis, Adams refused to recognize Hamilton as the commander in chief. With the war crisis at an end, Hamilton could only disband the army and resign, which he did in 1800. Hamilton had lost his direct influence in the government and his military command. Thereafter Hamilton and Adams were bitter enemies.

9. Politics Turn Deadly

Hamilton and the Federalist Party lost control of national politics after the elections of 1800. In the state elections, Hamilton campaigned fiercely for his party's candidates for the New York state assembly. However, the Republicans won easily. The state assemblies chose electors for the presidential elections. Because the Republican Party had control of the state's assembly, it was certain that the Republican presidential candidates, Thomas Jefferson and Aaron Burr, would win in New York. Burr ran the Republican campaign in that state and won a place on the presidential ticket for his good work.

At that time, the parties chose two candidates each, but no distinction was made between the presidential and the vice presidential contenders. The candidate who received the most electoral votes became president. The runner-up, regardless of party, became vice president. The Federalists chose incumbent John Adams and a southerner, Charles Pinckney, for their ticket. Holding a grudge against Adams, Hamilton urged the Federalists to vote in favor of Pinckney for president, even though a party majority favored Adams. Hamilton's position created a damaging split within the Federalist Party.

Partly because of the turmoil Hamilton had caused in his party, the Republicans won the election. Jefferson and Burr ended up tied with the most electoral votes. It was up to Congress to vote on who would be president and vice president.

Once again Hamilton opposed his own party. The Federalists preferred Aaron Burr to Jefferson. To everyone's surprise, Hamilton supported Jefferson. He tried desperately to persuade Federalist congressmen to vote for Jefferson instead of Burr. After several tied ballots, one Federalist gave in to Hamilton and threw out his vote, making Jefferson president and Burr vice president.

Aaron Burr, pictured here in a 1794 portrait by Gilbert Stuart, was one of Hamilton's political rivals. Ultimately Burr and Hamilton's disagreements would be fatal.

Why did Hamilton prefer Jefferson, his political enemy, to his fellow New Yorker, Burr? Hamilton simply felt that Jefferson was the lesser of two evils. Although he disagreed with Jefferson's policies, he believed that Jefferson posed no threat to the public welfare. On the other hand, Hamilton had greatly distrusted Burr from the very beginning of the party struggle. Burr showed up in national politics as a member of the Republican Party and an opponent of Hamilton's policies. Robert Troupe had written to Hamilton about the activities of Burr and the Republicans back in 1791, "If they succeed, they will tumble the . . . government in ruins to the ground." Another friend reported from New York, "[Burr] is avowedly your enemy, and stands pledged to his party for a reign of vindictive declamation against your measures." Hamilton saw Burr as a schemer who would endanger the country for his own gain.

After helping defeat Burr's presidential bid in the 1800 election, Hamilton focused on his private life. He built a house in Harlem, which was then a rolling countryside an hour's carriage ride from his Manhattan law office. He was also very busy as one of New York's most sought-after attorneys. Nonetheless politics was never far from his mind. In 1802, he started a newspaper, the *New-York Evening Post*, as an outlet for his political opinions. The *New York Post* exists to this day. It has been continuously published longer than any other newspaper in the country.

The 1804 elections brought Hamilton back onto the political scene. Jefferson and Burr did not get along, so

Hamilton built a country home in Harlem and called it The Grange.
This home, pictured in this 1804 engraving, provided an out-of-
town retreat from the hectic life of Hamilton's law practice.
Designed by architect John McComb Jr., the Federal style home
on 32 acres (13 ha) of land was completed in 1802.

the president saw to it that Burr was removed from the
Republican ticket. Burr had his eye on the New York gov-
ernor's race. Because he had been outcast by the
Republicans, Burr switched sides and ran as a Federalist.

Hamilton tried to rally the Federalists against Burr.
He used his usual argument that Burr could not be
trusted with power. He was also alarmed by news that
Burr had met with a group of Federalists from New
England that wanted the northern states to secede from
the union. Hamilton, who opposed the movement, feared

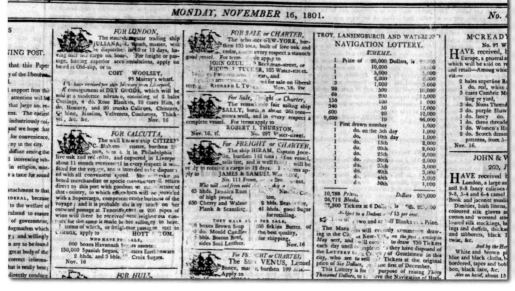

Hamilton founded the *New-York Evening Post* at the end of 1801 after his flurry of activity in the 1800 presidential election. He continued to write his opinions and was a powerful voice on the national political scene. This is the first edition, published on November 16, 1801.

that Burr might involve New York in the plot. This time Hamilton's arguments were ignored. The New York Federalists supported Burr. The Republican opposition was stronger, however, and their candidate won by a large margin. Nevertheless Burr held Hamilton responsible for his loss. Angry and humiliated, his political career in ruins, Burr challenged Hamilton to a duel.

Dueling was a ritual by which men settled personal disputes, usually when someone felt that his public reputation had been damaged. At that time, dueling was generally frowned upon. However, military men and men of the upper classes, mainly in the southern states, continued to uphold the tradition.

Duelists followed a strict code of rules. The offended party would issue a challenge through a go-between, called a second. It was up to the recipient to offer an apology or accept the challenge. If the challenge was accepted, the two would meet at a specific time and place for an interview, which is the code word for a duel. Because pistols were not very accurate at that time, it was not unusual for both duelists to walk

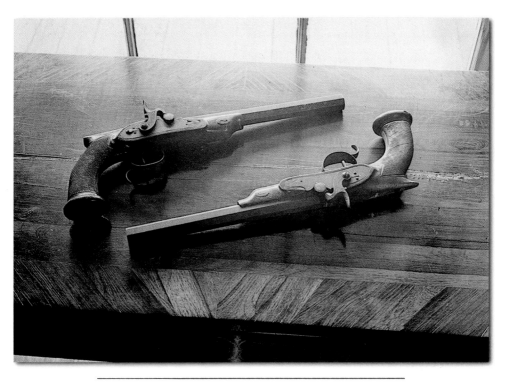

Special dueling pistols were used to resolve disputes with honor. Because the practice was so common in early America, wealthier individuals often owned a pair of matched pistols, such as the ones above.

The death of Hamilton, shown in this nineteenth-century hand-colored woodcut by Hooper, ended Burr's political career. The nation was shocked. Burr left his post as vice president in disgrace.

away uninjured, or with minor wounds, after shots were fired. Sometimes, though, the result was deadly.

Hamilton had been involved in a number of duels in his lifetime as both a challenger and a second. Most of the time, peace was achieved before shots were fired. In 1802, Hamilton's oldest son, Philip, was killed in a duel. The event devastated Hamilton, and he claimed afterward that he opposed the practice of dueling. Nevertheless when Burr demanded an explanation for a "despicable opinion" Hamilton reportedly gave of him during a speech in Albany, Hamilton did not apologize. He instead admitted that he had spoken harshly against Burr. Hamilton felt he had no choice but to accept Burr's challenge, although he regretted being a "bad example." It was important to him to uphold his opinions and to defend his honor on the dueling ground.

The duelists chose Weehawken, New Jersey, for their interview, because dueling was illegal in New York. On July 11, 1804, Burr and Hamilton, along with their seconds and a doctor, crossed the Hudson River in separate boats. The duel was finished in minutes. They measured off ten paces, and each fired a shot. Hamilton fell

This scene entitled *View of the Spot Where General Hamilton Fell at Weehawk* was created in 1830 to show the place where Hamilton was killed at Weehawken, New Jersey. Jacob C. Ward painted the engraving that was done by Caleb Ward.

immediately. Burr's bullet had hit him in the side and had lodged in his spine. The doctor managed to revive Hamilton, who diagnosed his own wound as fatal. He was brought to a friend's house in Manhattan, where he died the next day, on July 12, at 2:00 P.M. Betsey and their seven children were at his side.

Some claimed that Hamilton gave up his life to end Burr's political career. If this is true, he certainly achieved his goal. The duel stunned the nation. It stirred up an angry outcry against dueling and against Burr. Burr was indicted for murder in New York and in New Jersey. After giving a farewell speech to Congress, the disgraced vice president fled. A few years after the duel, Burr was tried for treason for attempting to lead an invasion into Spanish territory in Louisiana. After he was acquitted, he moved to Europe.

The nation mourned the loss of Alexander Hamilton. Although his reputation as a statesman had become damaged during his final years, his death brought back memories of his many achievements. Thousands of people, many weeping, lined the streets of Manhattan to watch his funeral procession. He was buried at Trinity Church on Broadway at Wall Street. His grave can still be visited today.

10. Hamilton's Legacy

One of Alexander Hamilton's greatest fears later in his life was that President Jefferson would dismantle Hamilton's financial system. He did not need to worry, however. His vision and legacy lasted long into the Jefferson administration and beyond.

As president, Jefferson not only maintained Hamilton's program, but also adopted some of his former rival's ideas. Jefferson kept the national bank, and even borrowed from it on a few occasions. Commerce and the stock trade, which Jefferson once strongly opposed, continued to flourish under his presidency. Jefferson would not tamper with the success of Hamilton's program. "Go where you will," Robert Troupe wrote, "you behold nothing but the smiling face of improvements and prosperity!" Although Hamilton and other Federalists waited gloomily for Jefferson to destroy their system, he made few changes.

Hamilton's doctrine of implied powers became an important tool for interpreting the Constitution throughout American history. Although Jefferson wrote

A timeworn Hamilton was sketched by friend Gordon Fairman from memory in 1805, a year after Hamilton's death. This is what he looked like around the time of his duel with Burr.

the argument against it while secretary of state, he ended up using Hamilton's doctrine as president to argue for the Louisiana Purchase. In 1819, implied powers were confirmed by the Supreme Court and used by future presidents to pass innovative laws.

Hamilton was also a groundbreaking attorney. In the famous appeals court case *Croswell v. the United States*, Hamilton fought for the freedom of the press. He defended a small newspaper publisher who was sued for libel because an article he published was critical of the government. At that time, libel law did not allow evidence of truth to be presented in court. This greatly restricted the

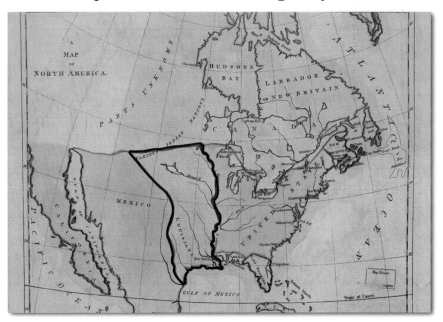

Jefferson used Hamilton's implied powers doctrine to argue in support of the Louisiana Purchase. The lands acquired, outlined in blue on this 1803 map, stretched from the Mississippi River to the Rocky Mountains and from the Gulf of Mexico to the Canadian border. The Louisiana Purchase nearly doubled the size of the United States, making it one of the largest nations in the world.

freedom of journalists, who feared such lawsuits. Hamilton argued forcefully that the if a newspaper's story was true it must be allowed to print it and to defend itself in court. He said it was the only way to ensure the freedom of the press. If such restrictions on journalists remained, Hamilton warned, "you must forever remain ignorant of what your rulers do." Although Hamilton lost the case, the state of New York eventually reconsidered the decision. The truth defense was made law in 1805 and was added to the state constitution sixteen years later. Hamilton's law-school study manual, *Practical Proceedings in the Supreme Court of New York*, became a standard authority on law practice in New York.

Hamilton helped create other lasting institutions as well. The Bank of New York still exists as that state's oldest bank. When a small group of New Yorkers created an association to make trading in U.S. government bonds easier, the New York Stock Exchange was born. The New York Stock Exchange remains the world's center of finance today. American-style capitalism, which Hamilton defined, has spread across the world.

Yet, in spite of his many accomplishments, Alexander Hamilton remained unappreciated for a long time. The other Founding Fathers left behind great statements on liberty, while Hamilton dealt with the practical workings of finance and government. Hamilton toiled over account books and legal briefs.

That image is not as inspiring as, for instance, Patrick Henry crying out "Give me liberty or give me death!" Hamilton's image suffered for a long time, as well, because historians tended to take Jefferson's side in the rivalry between Jefferson and Hamilton. While Jefferson was portrayed as the defender of liberty, Hamilton's efforts to strengthen the federal government were seen as tyrannic; that view has changed in recent times.

Hamilton was one founding member of the New York Stock Exchange, an institution that continues to thrive with the idea of commerce that Hamilton promoted.

Today the stock market and other matters of global finance affect everyday lives. The brilliance and the farsightedness of Hamilton's policies are much better appreciated, because more people understand these issues. Historians now view Hamilton in a more positive light, and people today are likely to think of him as a man who was ahead of his time.

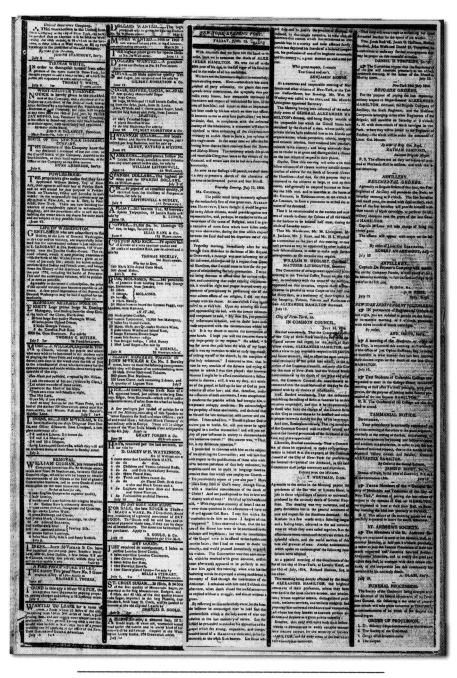

Alexander Hamilton's obituary, outlined in orange, in the
New-York Evening Post on July 13, 1804, reported the events of the
duel and the sorrow that news of Hamilton's death brought to
those who knew him. Hamilton's ideas were forward thinking,
and the far-reaching effects of his work are seen worldwide.

Above is Hamilton's memorial or mourning kerchief. A mourning kerchief was a traditional cotton handkerchief that had images and words printed on it about the well-known person who had passed away.

Although Alexander Hamilton does not have a monument in Washington, D.C., his quiet gravesite at Trinity Church in Manhattan is a fitting memorial. The grave and the church remain largely unchanged since Hamilton was buried in 1804, but the city has grown steadily all around them. The skyscrapers of the financial district now dwarf the church's stately spire. The national prosperity and the power represented by these buildings is the vision for which Hamilton argued throughout his career. It can be said that Hamilton is surrounded by the evidence of his lasting legacy.

Timeline

1755 or 1757	Alexander Hamilton is born.
1768	Alexander Hamilton's mother dies.
1769	Alexander Hamilton's first known letter is written.
1772	Hamilton arrives in New York.
1773	The Boston Tea Party occurs.
1774	Hamilton joins the New York militia.
1775	The American Revolution begins.
1776	The Declaration of Independence is signed.
	Washington leads a successful attack on a Hessian outpost at Trenton.
1777	Hamilton becomes aide-de-camp to General George Washington.
1778	France enters the American Revolution.
1780	Alexander Hamilton and Elizabeth Schuyler are married.
1781	Hamilton quits Washington's headquarters.

Hamilton begins to work on "The Continentalist" series.

Hamilton helps lead an assault on Yorktown.

1782   Hamilton is appointed the New York delegate to the Continental Congress.

1783   The Treaty of Paris is signed.

Hamilton argues the *Rutgers v. Waddington* case in court.

1786   Hamilton is elected to the New York assembly.

1787   Constitutional Convention is held in Philadelphia, Pennsylvania.

Hamilton works on "The Federalist" with John Jay and James Madison.

1788   New York ratifies the Constitution.

1789   George Washington is inaugurated president of the United States.

Hamilton takes office as secretary of the treasury on September 11.

1790   The first *Report on Public Credit* is submitted to Congress.

	The national capital moves to Philadelphia, Pennsylvania.
1791	Hamilton submits a report on the constitutionality of a national bank.
1795	Hamilton resigns from the Treasury.
1796	Hamilton drafts President Washington's farewell address.
1798	In the war crisis with France, Hamilton is appointed inspector general of the army by Washington.
1799	George Washington dies.
1800	Hamilton resigns as inspector general of the army.
	Washington, D.C., becomes the national capital.
1801	Work begins on the Grange, Hamilton's country house.
	Philip Hamilton, age 20, is killed in a duel.
1802	The Hamiltons move to the Grange.
1804	Hamilton and Burr duel on July 11.
	Hamilton dies on July 12.

Glossary

aide-de-camp (ayd-dih-KAMP) A military officer on the personal staff of a higher ranking officer.

Articles of Confederation (AR-tih-kuhls UV kuhn-feh-duh-RAY-shuhn) The first constitution of the United States, which lasted from March 1781 to June 1788.

artillery (ar-TIH-luh-ree) The branch of an army that specializes in using cannons.

assumption (uh-SUHMP-shuhn) The plan for the U.S. federal government to take responsibility for the unpaid wartime debts of individual states.

bankruptcy (BANK-ruhp-see) When a person or a group does not have enough money to pay its debts.

bond (BAHND) An interest-bearing certificate issued by a company or a government promising to pay the value of the certificate at a certain time.

boycott (BOY-kaht) Refusal to use or to buy goods as a form of protest.

brink (BRINK) The edge of something.

checks and balances (CHEHKS AND BA-lehns-ez) The system within the U.S. government in which each branch can control or check the power of the others so no branch becomes too powerful.

credit (KREH-diht) Confidence in the ability of a person, a company, or a government to pay its debts.

currency (KUHR-ehn-see) Money.

direct taxes (duh-REKT TAKS-ez) Taxes that come directly from the tax payer to the government.

divine right (duh-VYN RYT) The belief that kings and queens receive their right to rule directly from God.

duties (DOO-teez) A tax, especially on imports.

embargo (ehm-BAR-go) A ban on trade with a foreign nation, usually handed down by government.

Enlightenment (ihn-LY-tuhn-muhnt) A philosophical movement of the eighteenth century that used reason to challenge longstanding traditions.

excise (EHK-syz) A tax on the consumption, the production, or the sale of goods within a country, usually on luxuries or on unnecessary items.

faction (FAK-shun) A group with a particular interest that often puts it at odds with other groups.

illegitimate (il-lih-JIH-tuh-muht) Born of parents who are not married to each other.

implied powers doctrine (ihm-PLYD POW-uhrs DOK-truhn) A principle that states Congress has powers in addition to those directly spelled out in the Constitution.

interest (IHN-truhst) A fee charged for the use of money.

inviolate (ihn-VY-uh-luht) Not corrupted or dirtied.

Jacobin (JA-kuh-buhn) A member of an extremist political group that advocated equal rights for all and that engaged in terrorist activities during the French Revolution.

laird (LAYRD) The Scottish form of lord.

legislature (LEH-jus-lay-cher) An organized group having the power to make laws.

liaison (lee-AY-zon) An agent who maintains communication and unity between parts of an armed force.

manumission (muhn-yuh-MIH-shuhn) Freedom from slavery.

mediocrity (mee-dee-AH-kruh-tee) The state of being of only average or ordinary quality.

outpost (OWT-post) A post staffed with soldiers placed at a distance from the main branch of an army.

prominent (PRAH-muh-nehnt) Well-known.

ratify (RA-tuh-fy) To give formal approval.

regiment (REH-juh-mehnt) A military unit commanded by a colonel.

revenue (REH-vuh-noo) A source of income.

secede (sih-SEED) To withdraw membership from an organization, an association, or an alliance.

securities (seh-KYOOR-ih-tees) Certificates showing that money is owed to the bearer.

speculator (SPEH-kyeh-lay-ter) Someone who makes a risky investment with the hope of a large gain.

statesman (STAYTS-min) A person actively involved in the business of government or the shaping of its policies.

stocks (STAHKS) Certificates showing a person's ownership of shares in a company.

strict constructionism (STRIKT kon-STRUK-shuh-nih-zuhm) Principle in American constitutional law that Congressional power is limited to what is expressly stated in the Constitution.

Tory (TOR-ee) A nickname, usually negative in intent, given to people who support the policies of a monarchy.

treasonous (TREE-zuhn-uhs) Involving the attempt to overthrow the government.

Additional Resources

Books

Collier, Christopher and James Lincoln Collier. *Building a New Nation: The Federalist Era*. New York: Benchmark Books, 1999.

Hakim, Joy. *From Colonies to Country (History of Us, Book 3)*. New York: Oxford University Press, 1998.

Hamilton, Alexander. *Selected Writings and Speeches of Alexander Hamilton*. Ed. Morton J. Frisch. Washington and London: American Enterprise Institute for Public Policy Research, 1985.

Hamilton, Alexander, John Jay, and James Madison. *The Federalist Papers*. Ed. G. Wills. New York: Bantam, 1982.

Web Sites

http://memory.loc.gov/const/fed/fedpapers.html

www.lib.virginia.edu/exhibits/church/federal.html

www.pbs.org/wgbh/amex/duel/

Bibliography

Brookhiser, Richard. *Alexander Hamilton: American*. New York: The Free Press, 1999.

Cunningham, Noble E. *Jefferson vs. Hamilton*. New York: Bedford/St. Martins, 2000.

Elkins, Stanley, and E. McKitrick. *The Age of Federalism*. New York: Oxford University Press, 1993.

Emery, Noemie. *Alexander Hamilton: An Intimate Portrait*. New York: G.P. Putnam's Sons, 1982.

Fleming, Thomas. *Duel: Alexander Hamilton, Aaron Burr and the Future of America*. New York: Basic Books, 1999.

Hamilton, Alexander, James Madison, and John Jay. *The Federalist Papers*. Ed. G. Wills. New York: Bantam, 1982.

Hamilton, Alexander. *The Papers of Alexander Hamilton*. Ed. J. Cooke and H. Syrett. New York: Columbia University Press, 1961–87.

Hamilton, Alexander. *Selected Writings and Speeches of Alexander Hamilton*. Ed. Morton J. Frisch. Washington and London: American Enterprise Institute for Public Policy Research, 1985.

Index

About the Author

Lisa DeCarolis is the coordinator of Student Computing Services at Smith College, where she received her undergraduate degree in history. Her research into the American founding period led her to contribute a biography of Alexander Hamilton to the American History Hypertext Project of the University of Groningen, Netherlands. Inquiries from readers of that essay have prompted her to continue her explorations of Hamilton and the genealogy of his descendants and to visit many sites associated with Hamilton. This is her first book.

Credits

Photo Credits

Cover: Courtesy Independence National Historical Park (Portrait); National Archives (U.S. Constitution)

p. 4 © U.S. Mint; p. 7 courtesy Dover Books; p. 9 © National Archives and Records Administration; p. 12 © Library of Congress Geography and Map Division Washington, D.C. 20540-4650 USA, G4390 1774 .S62 Vault Oversize; pp. 14, 39 courtesy Columbia University Libraries, Hamilton Collection; p. 15 © Tony Roberts/CORBIS; pp. 18, 90 © NorthWind Pictures; pp. 22–23, 25, 91 courtesy the Phelps Stokes Collection, Miriam and Ira D. Wallach Division of Art, Prints, and Photographs, the New York Public Library, Astor Lenox, and Tilden Foundations; pp. 25, 27, 52, 78 courtesy Rare Books and Manuscripts, the New York Public Library, Astor Lenox, and Tilden Foundations; p. 29 courtesy Emmet Collection, Miriam and Ira D. Wallach Division of Art, Prints, and Photographs, New York Public Library, Astor Lenox, and Tilden Foundations; p. 33 courtesy Winterthur Museum; pp. 34, 56, 61 © Independence National Historical Park; pp. 36–37, 76, 83 © Bettmann/CORBIS; p. 38 photograph courtesy of Charles Penniman; pp. 40, 55, 62, 94, 98, 99 collection of the New-York Historical Society; p. 43 © CORBIS; p. 46 © National Portrait Gallery, Smithsonian Institution/Art Resource, NY; pp. 47, 48, 65 © Museum of the City of New York; p. 58 © Library of Congress Manuscript Division; pp. 61, 69, 76 courtesy Independence National Historical Park; p. 67 courtesy the Robert H. Gore, Jr. Numismatic Collection, Department of Special Collections, University of Notre Dame Libraries; pp. 71, 87 © Culver Pictures; p. 82 photograph courtesy of the Fenimore Art Museum, Cooperstown, New York; p. 85 courtesy collections of the New Jersey Historical Society, Newark, NJ; p. 88 courtesy the New York Post; p. 89 © Archive Photos; p. 95 © Library of Congress Geography and Map Division; p. 97 © Dallas and John Heaton/CORBIS.

Editor
Joanne Randolph

Series Design
Laura Murawski

Layout Design
Corinne Jacob

Photo Researcher
Jeffrey Wendt